Lord Deliver Me From People is a work that is ordained by God to be a word to leaders and the Body of Christ. Bishop Reeves, a humble and powerful servant of God, has impacted the Church worldwide. He is a Shepherd, but he, like David, is also a man after God's own heart. He is a man that is changing culture and society and how we look at family and our relationships within and without. It is a book that every one needs who enjoys relationships. A page turner!

Judy Jacobs Tuttle
Pastor, Worship Leader, Author, Mentor

Bishop Eugene Reeves has expressed his heart in *Lord Deliver Me from People: Navigating the Relationships that Disrupt Your Life*. As a seasoned pastor, successful leader, and family advocate, Bishop Reeves strategically teaches biblical foundations to bring godly balance and maturity in all our relationships. Amazing, powerful, enlightening, and life changing, are words that describe this great book; you will not be disappointed.

Pastor Jamie Tuttle
Dwelling Place Church International
Cleveland, Tennessee

I have known Eugene Reeves for years now. Besides being a valued colleague and a dear friend, he is a proven leader who, like Moses, has been caring for God's people for decades in relative obscurity. It is time now for him to emerge onto a broader stage and serve the nations. His writing is practical, while carrying a prophetic edge. *Lord, Deliver Me From People* is a book on self-deliverance for every person who has challenging relationships. This is a must read, and great research resource for your library, and an important training manual.

Bishop Harry R. Jackson, Jr.
Senior Pastor, Hope Christian Church
President, High Impact Leadership Coalition
Presiding Bishop of the International Communion of
Evangelical Churches

To succeed in this life, you must know people. The Stanford Research Institute found that the money you make in any endeavor is 12.5% product knowledge and 87.5% people knowledge. Bishop Reeves, an excellent leader in his own right, has a gift. He knows people. Not only can he teach us how to choose the right team members, and mentor and train protégés, he is also skilled in teaching us when and how to devalue cynical relationships and be delivered from cantankerous people.

Through eye opening experience coupled with rare heavenly insight, Bishop Reeves lifts our relational lid. You will be given permission to lovingly but respectfully "shake the dust off of your feet" and move on. This book is masterful but merciful. Read on…Liberation awaits!

Bishop Kyle Searcy
Senior Pastor, Fresh Anointing House of Worship

Lord,
DELIVER ME
FROM
PEOPLE!

Navigating the Relationships that
Disrupt Your Life

Eugene V. Reeves

ISBN: 978-1-4675-8579-8
Lord, Deliver Me From People
Copyright © Eugene V. Reeves,
Eugene V. Reeves Ministries
Woodbridge, VA

Cover design: Terry Clifton
Text Design: Lisa Simpson, Simpson Productions
Print Production: Gene Gregg, Precision Concepts

Dedication

This book is dedicated to my mother, the late Mrs. Artavia W. Reeves, of Forrest City, Arkansas. She was and continues to be a source of inspiration and wisdom to me in every area of my life. I learned more about loving people from my mother than any other person I have ever met. It was my mother that taught me the phrase "it does not cost a dime to be kind." She always emphasized to all of her sons to treat people like you want to be treated regardless of how they treat you. She taught me how to love the unlovable and how to love myself.

Acknowledgements

Many thanks to my wife Ollie and my children Latashia, Greg, Demetrius and Trina. I could not do what I do without your love and support. Thank you so much for your support. I love you all more than you will ever know.

To my wonderful New Life staff, you are the best. Thank you for all you do to support the mission of The Life.

A special thanks to Kathy and Jan; I could not have done it without all your support and motivation.

Contents

Foreword

Nothing about our human experience seems to be completely perfect — life is complex enough even before we throw relationships into the mix. We are challenged to develop and to grow in spite of the complexities inherent within each relationship we attempt to cultivate. Those to whom we attach ourselves are a part of the quest we find ourselves on in search of a mirrored image of who we are. Sadly, our journey carries us over rough social terrains as we interact with others, intimately, professionally, socially and spiritually. No man is an island; we were created for community. Overcoming difficulties and the emotional pain associated with the disappointments of our past demands that we face our present with the resolve to overcome the same.

Life is a kaleidoscopic contradiction. Our relationships with friends, spouses, colleagues, and family members can be wonderfully rewarding. Conversely, they can also bring heartache, frustration, and disappointment. We all know the ones that make us feel open, authentic and at ease. Equally we also are aware of those that make us guarded, defensive, and awkward.

Healthy, loving and mutually beneficial relationships are difficult to cultivate and maintain, but in spite of the challenges, they are nonetheless possible. Why are these kinds of relationships so difficult? To begin with, we come into relationships from different backgrounds and bring our life scripts with us — scripts that have been cultivated and reinforced by our socialization, education and culturalization experiences. Added to these dynamics are all the repressed emotions garnered from our childhood experiences. How we experienced love as a child provides us with the series of love lessons that we carry into adulthood. For instance, if we experienced constant fighting, screaming, yelling and belittlement in our family, what we might conclude is that relationships bring suffering and unhappiness. You might have seen one of your parents dominated and controlled by the other. Thus, in your relationships, this scene may play out in a repeated fashion — you either dominate or become dominated.

Sometimes, people develop negative thoughts about themselves as a result of the negativity they experienced within their family during their childhood. Why do we get trapped in negative emotions when it's clear that life is so much fuller and richer when we are free of them? One of the reasons is because no one has offered us an alternative pattern or model for us to follow.

The most important relationship lessons I learned is that the relationships we have with other people are projections of the relationships we have with ourselves. We do not draw to ourselves whom we want but who we are. It is an issue of like attracting like. Our external relationships and our internal relationships are in fact the same relationships. When we learn how to love ourselves, we attract people who love us equally. When we establish relationships with others, we are actually searching for a mirrored image of ourselves. This is why when we find something in common with another person, we get excited because that person is mirroring for us who we really are. Even many of the things we reject in others, we actually secretly harbor in ourselves.

Bishop Reeves book, *Lord Deliver Me From People: Navigating The Relationships That Disrupt Your Life*, is a practical discourse that examines the challenges we encounter with our relationships and explores the remedies by addressing their root causes. Sharing his personal experiences, sound biblical principles and the next steps to take toward wholeness, his wisdom from years of counseling and training gives us hope that we can break free from these negative experiences. He gives us principles to help reshape our viewpoint of ourselves as well as those around us. He also explores the fact that the things we don't like about our relationships are all within our power to change, when we have the courage to change ourselves and adjust our expectations of others, we will also have the ability to see the part we play in them so that we can grow beyond them.

This is not a book that merely provides solutions, instead it shows how we can put ourselves in a receptive mode to discover and find truths on our own as we establish an authentic relationship with God. Brilliantly written, simply stated and filled with riveting stories that we all can identify with, this book is a must-read.

Cindy Trimm,
author, minister and trusted voice of hope

Chapter I

When Knowing You is Defining Me

"The applause of a single human being has great consequences."[1]
—*Samuel Johnson*

Everyone has at least one hero. Mine was my father. He was a First Sergeant in the 82nd Airborne during the Vietnam Era, which made him a pretty tough guy. I had always looked up to my dad, his crisp uniform and military demeanor as well as the respect he commanded both on post and around the church community. We were living in Forrest City, Arkansas, my parents' hometown that was at the heart of segregation and race riots. I played in the all-black Babe Ruth League baseball team and excelled in home runs and batting percentage. But I wanted to play in a better league — an all-white club — on the other side of town. As I excitedly told my father about the try-outs, he was surprisingly negative. He told me to just stay with our league and to leave well enough alone.

---

[1] *Life of Johnson*, Volume 4 1780-1784, James Boswell 2012 Amazon Digital Book.

I was undaunted and went with a friend to the try-outs anyway. We were the only two African-American kids on the entire field. They had to let us try out but they had no intention of allowing us to make the team. My fielding was pretty good that day; they had to notice my gift. When it came time to bat, I was the only player during tryouts to hit a home run as well as several hits. My friend had also done well and we eagerly waited for them to announce the names for who had made the team. Both of us were extremely disappointed when we were told that we were not skilled enough to make this league.

I was angry. I knew I played much better than many of the white kids that made the team. I realized that the color of my skin was the deciding factor. So, I brought the injustice to my dad's attention. I complained about how my friend and I were mistreated. I knew he would defend me...he would march over to the coach's house and right this wrong. He would stand up for me. He would never let me miss this opportunity.

I was shocked when my dad reminded me that he had asked me not to go in the first place. He told me I should not have tried out at all. He said there was nothing he could do about it so I needed to forget it. I was devastated. I couldn't believe that my father, who commanded so much respect in so many places, would cop out so easily. I felt that he had failed me. This event was a double hurt for me: first, from the white establishment and second from my father. I would not be the next Jackie Robinson!

Making the Grade

When I was growing up, I constantly sought the approval of my father, but I never really got it. I love my father and now I don't blame him for not giving me his "okay." You see, my father didn't know how to approve of me because he himself had never received approval. You have to understand that my father was the oldest of ten children and my grandfather, whom I never met, died suddenly of a stroke when my father was just seventeen years old. My father had to assume the leadership and responsibility of the family as well as the farm where they lived. The youngest of the children was only a couple of months old. No wonder my father never understood how to affirm me or my brothers — his father never had time to affirm him. The only take-away he received from his dad was to work hard and take care of the family; these were the same words and advice that my father passed on to me. Although nothing is wrong with a strong work ethic, being a great dad is more than just providing for your family. Emotional bonding through approval and affirmation is just as important for fathers to convey to their kids. Lack of approval seems to plague many of the people I have met throughout the years — both men and women. It often affects them physically, emotionally and spiritually.

> When I was growing up, I constantly sought the approval of my father.

15

I spent much of my time searching for my father to validate me as a man. Do you remember times when you sought approval but it eluded you? The need for approval from people is just one of many issues that makes our relationships fall flat. The need for acceptance also claims many victims. Acceptance slightly differs from approval. Approval validates what you do and how you act by showing support, while acceptance validates who you are as a person.

Another issue for many folks is the need to be needed. Unless they are helping make a difference in some fashion, they feel inadequate. What is so very sad is that I had all three issues in my life. The need for approval, the need to be accepted and the need to be needed controlled much of who I was. It took time and work to feel delivered from these needs, but I feel my struggle is not unlike many of yours.

Many Christians sit in church and still struggle with multiple needs. These needs are like addictions to drugs or alcohol because they numb the senses and create deadly issues simultaneously causing dysfunction in the people around them. Over the years, I have seen people going on for decades without knowing why they act a certain way and why they treat situations or relationships with specific unhealthy reactions.

This book was written because many people have told me they can identify with my problems as being similar to their own. But more than that, I believe my story didn't end at the problem stage. It rose through a period of deliverance into a realm of victory. This victory is available to every Christian. So let's get to work!

My problems started as a young child. I felt like the guinea pig. I felt like I was the "experimental" African-American student. In the late 50s, I was in an all-white kindergarten class and it always seemed that I was the focus of attention, but only for the wrong reasons. In first and second grade my teachers were white, and this theme seemed to continue. Although I was the only child with black skin, they tried to be very fair with me. The pinnacle came in third grade; I had a teacher that was 6 feet tall with blue eyes and blonde hair, she looked like a WWF wrestler — broad shoulders, big muscles and tough. She totally intimidated me. No, she didn't physically harm me but the words she said to me did hurt me psychologically and almost ruined my childhood.

For example, when she would give all the kids in the classroom an assignment and class work on the board, she would give me paper and crayons and tell me to color. Imagine — they were doing problems and learning math while I was coloring! I remembered times when I would take a crayon and begin to write the numbers from the chalkboard. If the teacher caught me doing this, she would verbally admonish me for trying to do the math problems. How could I, a little kid, fight what was happening?

This teacher told my mother and the principal that I would never learn like the other children, that I was slow, and needed to be in a special school. My mom had never finished school so she believed everything that she was told by those in authority. Therefore, I went through that entire year completely beaten down emotionally. By the time I finished that year, I believed I was stupid. I believed I could not learn. I believed I was just ignorant. For years, I never realized why I had such a dislike for people who reminded me of this teacher; this unfair treatment had developed into an issue. Now I was prejudiced against people that reminded me of her physically without realizing why.

One day, my father came home from work and informed the family that once again he was being sent to Vietnam. He also told my mother that this time we could not remain in on-post housing but had to move off post or return to their hometown of Forrest City, AR. They both thought it would be best to be around family and friends, so we packed up and moved to Arkansas.

During that fourth grade year, there was a beautiful young teacher by the name of Ms. Janice J. Jones — my first African-American teacher. She was very soft spoken, easy going, and very approachable. This teacher knew I was a new student in a new school in a new setting so she sat me right beside her desk so she kept a close eye on how I was adjusting to the new surroundings. This time the children didn't look at me like I was out of place. You see, it was the first segregated class I had ever attended. And there, in that all-black school, I discovered I wasn't stupid; I wasn't ignorant. Because I had been told for so long that I was slow, it took someone in authority — my fourth grade teacher — to let me know I had been smart all along.

I began to believe the encouraging words she spoke to me and every time I finished a paper or an assignment, I found it necessary to run up to her desk to hear that I had done everything correctly...that it was good...that it was okay. I believe the Lord put Ms. Jones in that school for that one year just for me, as she only taught there for one year. She didn't realize what had been said in the past or what the others had spoken into my life. I will never forget my mother's expression when Ms. Jones told my mother what an intelligent and well behaved student I was. "He's very bright, but for some reason I have to keep telling him that he's smart."

The lack of approval from my past had a residual effect — it created a dependency on needing someone to constantly give me affirmation and approval. Of course, none of them realized what I had been through, and I couldn't verbalize my needs because I was too young to cognitively understand what had happened to me. I needed people to tell me that they approved of what I did because I did not possess one crumb of self-esteem. I even was accused of being the teacher's pet because I had to go up to her desk to validate my work. I couldn't trust myself to do well because I had internalized the negative words that were said about me, even if I knew they were completely false.

Have you ever internalized something somebody said about you that was totally false? For example, somebody may have told you that you weren't a good person. Too many of us are running around wounded and hurting while trying to live a "normal life." This is because we have not been delivered from the hurt and pain of our past. The Apostle Paul talks about this in 1 Timothy 5:24, "*The sins of some are obvious, reaching the place of judgment ahead of them; the sins of others trail behind them.*" But Paul also encourages us that we can finish our race well, "*Brothers and sisters, I do not consider myself yet to have taken hold of it. But one thing I do: Forgetting what is behind and straining toward what is ahead*" (Philippians 3:13 NIV). This is the encouragement all of us need!

Outward Appearances as a Means of Acceptance

Many times, we focus on the outward things. We often spend the most time on our outward appearances and, in effect, we practice the art of cover-up. We believe if we look good, we will feel good, and no one will notice just how messed up we really feel. We then become overly concerned about how we look. Many women become overly obsessed about their physical appearance while men become overly preoccupied about what kind of car they drive. We believe that our image

> We believe if we look good, we will feel good, and no one will notice just how messed up we really feel.

20

becomes what others see. Consequently, how I feel becomes based on the outward life while inwardly we're still hurting. People may begin to use our need for approval and acceptance in order to control us. In essence, they imply that, if we don't please them, if we don't make them happy, then they're not happy with us. We see this often in the work place. We may have a boss who dumps all his/her work on the same person repeatedly. Why does that person allow the boss to use them time and time again? Maybe you know someone who has that kind of power over you. After many years of this type of treatment, we find that we're still suffering and we're still looking for something to calm the pain that never goes away.

If you've ever been hurt or wounded by people who are difficult — or even impossible — to please, you may think that God is the same way. We begin to fear that we can never please God, so we try to keep up outward appearances with Him. We work hard in a ministry that we perhaps are not supposed to do. We say and do the right "religious things" in order to make the grade. But it is impossible to please God...unless we have faith. *"But without faith it is impossible to please and be satisfactory to Him. For whoever would come near to God must [necessarily] believe that God exists and that He is the rewarder of those who earnestly and diligently seek Him [out]"* (Hebrews 11:6, Amplified).

It is futile to try to please God with mere outward appearance. Yet, so many of us work so hard at the appearance we forget the fact that He knows our frame! (See Psalm 139:15.)

Our acceptance and approval have been fully taken care of. God was not afraid to create us and He was definitely not afraid to find a way to make us acceptable to Him. He also had a plan to make us approved to spend eternity with Him.

> *"For this reason I bow my knees to the Father of our Lord Jesus Christ, from whom the whole family in heaven and earth is named, that He would grant you, according to the riches of His glory, to be strengthened with might through His Spirit in the inner man, that Christ may dwell in your hearts through faith; that you, being rooted and grounded in love, may be able to comprehend with all the saints what is the width and length and depth and height to know the love of Christ which passes knowledge; that you may be filled with all the fullness of God."*
>
> *Ephesians 3:14-19 NKJV*

Let's take a closer look at verses 16 and 17. He is going to grant us out of His riches of His treasury in glory. This is the best of the best! This rich treasury of His glory will be what strengthens us in the inner man — not a father's approval, not a teacher's approval, not acceptance based on outward appearances. This strength will reinforce us for those times when others don't accept us or deny us their approval.

The Holy Spirit Himself will dwell in our innermost being. His work is not just to "quicken" us to dance during worship or give a shout or say "hallelujah" during a sermon. We do an injustice to His work when we relegate the divine work of the Holy Spirit to such small signs. The Holy Spirit was given to strengthen and change our inner being. In other words, the Holy Spirit will allow us to become what we cannot be on our own.

SELAH:

Take a moment to digest what has been shared thus far. Use the verses in Ephesians that are written above as a prayer. Place your name in the context of the verses to personalize each statement. Earnestly seek the Father's heart as you pray in order to have a divine exchange...one that can set you on a new course toward how God sees you!

Recall I said previously I had negative reactions for years when I saw anyone who resembled my third-grade teacher. The enemy likes to use experiences from our childhood to set us up in our adult life to think and act according to a wrong pattern. We see this pattern in the physical abuse of children. Someone is beaten as a child and they end up beating their children. In your case, it could be an absentee father or maybe a mother who is physically at home but emotionally disengaged. These scars set us up to create lifelong addictions. An addiction is something that controls us. We think addictions are only to drugs, alcohol, food, etc. but this is not the case. Do you have a people addiction?

People addictions start when we develop the need to hear certain words in order to feel validated. People addictions set us up for a performance orientation. But God wants us to realize that He's pleased with us because we serve Him.

Here

Many of us can't receive this — we know God's Word says it, we know it is a truth in our heads, but our hearts haven't embraced this simple fact. It's too easy; it's difficult to break away from the addiction with people and we begin to see God in the same light. Just because man may be disappointed in you doesn't mean that God is. I am going to repeat this so it will sink in. Just because man may be disappointed in you doesn't mean that God is. And just because you haven't lived up to some standard that somebody has set for you doesn't mean that God is not pleased with you. In order to be delivered from a people addiction, the first thing you have to realize is that "if God is pleased with me, then I'm all right." Can you say that out loud to yourself right now? "I'm alright!"

> Just because man may be disappointed in you doesn't mean that God is.
>
> ❧

The only opinion that really matters is that God is pleased. Let me take you further down this path. Hebrews 11:6 says, "*But without faith it is impossible to please Him*" (NIV). So if I have faith, then it pleases God. God tells us that we really only need to have a childlike faith. That's enough faith to believe that He is. And if you have enough faith to believe that He exists, then you can have enough faith to trust what He says. He says that if you acknowledge Him in all your ways, He will direct your path. (See Proverbs 3:6.) Acknowledge first that He sent His Son to die as a substitute for you. If you have enough faith to believe His Son died for you and rose from the dead, you will be saved. Do you have enough faith to trust Him for your salvation? Do you believe that He's real? Do you believe that He is the author and the finisher of your faith? This "Finisher of the Faith" wants to get rid of everything that stands between you and the finish line.

Those who have been hurt badly through abuse or strict regimen often seek the approval of others to try to overcome their fear of rejection and low self-esteem. And if you've been abused or you've been rejected, approval and acceptance from others may stand in your way. Hearing that you are good or pretty or smart may be blocking your faith. Know that you don't have to be good or pretty or smart according to what another person sees. Just remember what God has said about you!

People who need approval or acceptance will do almost anything to gain the approval they feel they have lost. Recall the example of the boss who dumps work on the same employee over and over again. What does that employee do over and over again? They work harder and harder, trying to please the boss while telling themselves, "This time, if I work really really hard, I'll make my boss happy. I just know I will." This drive for approval taints every area of their lives. It becomes a long chain of decisions based on the need. It intrudes on relationships, career choices and ministry. They begin to adjust based on whether they will disappoint the boss or someone else in authority and therefore they will not receive any approval. Because this is an addiction to the approval and acceptance from others, they look for a "fix" whenever the situation becomes shaky. These quick fixes can come in different flavors — excessive behaviors such as using drugs, food, work, or shopping to stop the "shaking" have all been used to fix the empty spots in the lives of others.

Look at 2 Corinthians 5:21: *"For He made Him who knew no sin to be sin for us, that we might become the righteousness of God in Him"* (NKJV). Paul was saying that even though you may have an addiction or you may have a problem, there is an answer.

I found out the hard way that you can't replace Jesus. We can't shop enough, drink enough, change partners enough or get high enough to fix our problems. The answer is that Jesus allowed Himself to be made sin to pay the price for us that we may be the righteousness of Christ. So what did He do? He became our substitute. Do you know what that means? Christ knew what it meant to feel rejection from the lack of acceptance and approval. He knew the pain and the hurt of those closest to Him not understanding Him. He allowed Himself to feel every emotional hurt so that He might be The Answer for our hurt.

Isn't it ironic that we look to the very people for approval and acceptance who cannot ever deliver that which we need? He can't help you. She can't help you. It takes God to help you. I don't know what you're into right now, I don't know what you've been into in the past, I don't know what you will be into in the future, but whatever condition you might have doesn't start with drugs and it doesn't finish with a bottle. It doesn't start with another sexual partner; credit cards can't be the answer to it. The answer for you starts with a J and ends with an S. JESUS. He became sin that we might be free from sin.

Have you ever understood why the devil came at you the way he did? Have you ever wondered why you went through what you went through as a child? Have you ever questioned why you were born to the parents you had? Have you ever pondered why the events that took place happened specifically to you? Or are you reacting to your current spouse based on the words and hurts you experience from your ex-spouse? Many of us have never really ever dealt with the situations we went through in both our childhood and our adolescence. Many of us have tried to forget it, tried to move on, tried to push through it and press it down, but it hasn't worked.

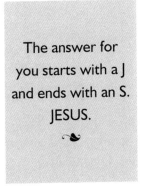

The answer for you starts with a J and ends with an S. JESUS.

Part of the reason we can't get to a place of freedom is because so many negatives keep arising in our lives to the point that we react based on what we've been through, and not where we are today. So often we react to other people based on our past because it triggers a former emotion or memory — like that of my disdain for people who looked like my third-grade teacher. And sadly, those people may never have done anything wrong to you. For example, you might be rejecting your current co-worker based on the experience you had with your ex-co-worker. I also have heard women declare, "No man will ever hurt me again." They have put their guard up against all men because of a negative past experience. But as they put their guard up, they also put up walls of distrust and shield their emotions. This is the same process that takes place when the abused person becomes the abuser. The person that got abused ends up becoming one who perpetrates the abuse they endured.

Another way we continue the cycles of rejection and pain is through our children. We often pass our fears on to our family members without intending to do so. Our kids live in a false world because of our insecurities. We tell ourselves that we are just protecting them but what we're actually doing is controlling them because we have not been delivered from our own issues. Our lives aren't normal. And, face it — our children's lives aren't normal either. We allow a painful incident or relationship from our past to have so much power over our current status that our entire family is in disarray. We have become people pleasers and when we turn around, we watch our children becoming the very same thing. They are just like Mom...just like Dad. And this is after telling ourselves over and over again that we will never be like them or we will never do what they did. Now our greatest fear has come true and we have become what we feared the most.

> Another way we continue the cycles of rejection and pain is through our children.

The plain truth is hard to swallow, but I am daring to tell it to you anyway. Truthfully, it was I who rejected myself when I was a kid. I didn't like myself. I didn't like the way I looked. I didn't like anything about me. I didn't hate myself but I didn't like myself. So consequently, I always needed somebody to like me but what I didn't know — and what I could not see — was how God saw me. I only saw how I thought other people saw me.

When I was about 4 years old, I got hit in the mouth with one of those old, iron playground swings. It broke my gums and eradicated all but one or two pieces of my teeth in the front of my mouth. Instead of the usual one year without front teeth, I had three years without them. Predictably, the kids began to call me names. I didn't want to open my mouth, nor did I want to smile or laugh. I didn't even want to talk. I didn't want to answer questions because everyone was going to have something to say about what they saw. Not only did I have the emotional pain from my former teacher, I also had a physical pain as my mouth was a mess. What I didn't realize was that God was working on the inside of me, but people only saw what they wanted to see.

Have you been called names? "Meat stick," "Fatso," "String bean." People may have called you bright names or dark names. They conjure up nappy-haired names, big-eyed names, four-eyed names; buck tooth, snaggle tooth, pigeon toed, knock-kneed…all kind of names. We may have even acted like we weren't bothered by the ridicule…the word "acted" is key here. We hear that, "Sticks and stones may break my bones. Words will never hurt me!" The truth is that I'd have rather been hit by a stick than hear the words that penetrated deep, because words do hurt.

Our daughters and our young men end up in bad situations because they're trying to find somebody who will love them just the way they are. How many movie stars or athletes do we read about each year who either have committed suicide or are slowly committing suicide by living a wild and dangerous lifestyle? Have you ever seen a smart young lady end up with an absolute dud for a spouse? How in the world can this happen? You see, this no-account, ugly-on-the-inside person said something to her at a vulnerable time — the time when she needed to hear words of approval and acceptance. His words were melodious to her aching soul and she clung to him because of her need.

> I'd have rather been hit by a stick than hear the words that penetrated deep, because words do hurt.
>
> ❧

How can we know if we are making right decisions in relationships? It is written plainly in the Word of God. "*For we are the circumcision, who worship God in the Spirit, rejoice in Christ Jesus, and have no confidence in the flesh, though I also might have confidence in the flesh. If anyone else thinks he may have confidence in the flesh, I more so*" (Philippians 3:3-4, NKJV).

Unless we have peace — the real peace of God, we cannot rely on our instincts or intuition to make the right choices. When we receive Christ, we are no longer to place our confidence in our flesh but in Him.

SELAH:

Take a moment to inventory your pattern of negative choices and feelings. Do you fall into the trap of having confidence in the flesh instead of in the Son of God? Ask God to replace these memories of the past and their attached feelings with the peace and joy of the Holy Ghost.

Performance Orientation

One of the most pervasive results of needing approval and acceptance is becoming performance-oriented. We have to do certain things in order to be validated. For example, I believed I was the best officer in the entire United States Army. I had to get an absolutely perfect Officer Evaluation Report (OER). Out of the 18 OER's that I received, only one was less than perfect. But I remember that one more than all the rest, because to me it said something was wrong with me. Later, I confronted the person that wrote that less than perfect OER. He told me what an outstanding officer I had become but if he did not write the truth about my performance, I would never improve in the areas that were lacking. Without his critique, I would believe nothing could improve. I now realize that my issue wasn't the job or the performance but because I needed to hear someone say that I was good at what I did. I still needed the father figure validation that I had never received as a child. I needed to see the written words of approval so I could read over and over just how good I was. And I'd work just that much harder so I could get the next report so I could again feel validated as a great soldier.

Too many times we end up performing in order to obtain the approval of someone else. We should be performing in an excellent manner as it reflects Christ, but instead we are just trying to get someone else to affirm us. That affirming addiction moves so deep in us that we pass it on to our children. We call it "perfectionism." We must be perfect and our children must echo our perfect lives. This way of performance leads strictly to a dead end.

> Too many times we end up performing in order to obtain the approval of someone else.

One of the sure signs you've got this condition is that every time you look at yourself in the mirror, you see what is wrong with you. Each time you look inside yourself, you see what's missing and what you don't have. Have you ever known somebody who has everything — wealth, a beautiful family, a great career — and yet it still isn't enough? That's because the true problem doesn't have to do with what you possess.

But I do have great news…you are really okay. It doesn't matter who mom was. It doesn't matter that dad left when you were two years old. All that matters is that God had a purpose for your life and the reason you're alive now is because God has ordained you to be here.

But that isn't enough…I've got even more good news for you! Not only are you alive for God's purposes and kingdom, but God has deliverance awaiting you. Once you come into the knowledge of who you are, you no longer need to live for people; you are living for God. And as long as your God is happy with you, it doesn't matter what people may think about you.

This truth became real for me as I grew older and older and studied the Word of God. I found out that I was valuable by who I was in Christ. As a matter of fact, I found out I was precious — a son of the Most High God! I discovered that I was valuable in His sight. And it had nothing to do with what I did. It didn't matter what career I chose. It didn't matter what other people's opinion of me was. My insecurity began to melt away and suddenly I no longer just saw my flaws, I began to see my abilities.

Taking this need for affirmation a bit further, there are those who feel like they have a "Kick Me" sign on their back. When you need somebody to love you, the devil's going to make sure you always feel rejected. Have you ever noticed that when you have this condition, it is all-inclusive — it seems like everybody dislikes you! But people are not the enemy. The devil is the one always against you, trying to magnify the bad and make it look like everybody hates you. But when you know who you are in Christ Jesus, it no longer matters what the world thinks. It matters what I know — and I know who I am in Christ Jesus. Do you know who you are?

"Christ's life showed me how, and enabled me to do it. I identified myself completely with him. Indeed, I have been crucified with Christ. My ego is no longer central. It is no longer important that I appear righteous before you or have your good opinion, and I am no longer driven to impress God. Christ lives in me. The life you see me living is not "mine," but it is lived by faith in the Son of God, who loved me and gave himself for me"

Galatians 2:20 MSG

If we were put on this planet to achieve, then we would be called achievers and not believers. God didn't call us achievers because we're supposed to have faith. Achievers have fear and not faith — a fear that they won't measure up. Let me tell you the difference between faith and fear. Faith is believing in God. Fear is believing what the devil says. The moment you fear means that you believe the enemy rather than God. Every time a fear comes into my mind, I have to tell the devil that he is a liar. I must realize that anything that comes into my mind that doesn't produce faith or a positive reaction must be rebuked immediately! I can have no room for doubt — I need faith to be in front of me, behind me, over me and under me. I have to live, eat and walk by faith. I need faith to carry me to my next place in God.

I know my Lord loves me. I know He's on my side and that's all that matters. Hebrews 12:2a says, *"looking unto Jesus, the author and finisher of our faith*" (NKJV). This verse tells us that if we're going to walk with God, we must look away from everything that is distracting us. We don't have time for foolishness. If someone has an attitude with us, we need to let them have their attitude but we don't have time to deal with it. It is distracting us from our Savior and taking precious time away from achieving our purpose in the earth.

Every time I think of Jesus' goodness and from where He has brought me, I am amazed. I used to live my life to please everybody. Can you imagine a pastor being a people pleaser? Nothing would ever get done in the church because each person has a set of changing needs and so every time you see them, you would have another new thing to do. A pastor becomes pulled in 90 different directions trying to please everybody.

I thank God for my liberty; to only desire that God is pleased with me. That doesn't mean I don't care for people. I just have come to understand that relationships are not based on how I perform but based on who I am. We must stop performing — putting on a show and just be real in Christ Jesus. This is the foundation step to be delivered from people!

> A pastor becomes pulled in 90 different directions trying to please everybody.
> ❧

Questions for Thought:

1. Have you identified with any of the behaviors that Bishop Reeves has mentioned in this chapter? If so, what are they?

2. Are there specific ways you cope with a sense of rejection or lack of affirmation? (Like shopping or eating, etc.) How can you recognize these and stop medicating your pain through these sources?

3. Have you learned to accept what God has given to you? Or do you actually like feeling the pain of rejection and nurse it?

SELAH:

If you answered the questions above and, while you did so, began to think of other people and their issues rather than yourself and your own issues, take a courageous step forward and ask God to take the logs out of your eyes so you can see your blind spots. Close your eyes and lift your hands before the Lord. Allow your hurting heart to be exposed to the Lord. He can be trusted to be tender toward you. Release the pain of the past. Release insecurities about how God has made you. And get ready for the next step to becoming free!

Chapter 2

When Helping You is Hurting Me

"You need to stop doing things for someone when you find out it's expected rather than appreciated."

—*Unknown*

Life is filled with opportunities to help other people, but the challenge is to know the difference between being helpful and being used. A few months after Ollie and I were married, I had a cousin ask if she and her husband could stay with us for a couple of weeks until they found somewhere to live. They were in a bad place. My wife and I were very young at the time and did not think much about it. We only had a one-bedroom apartment and all we could offer was the living room couch and the floor. Little did we know that the couple of weeks would turn into a six-month fiasco that was filled with drama and issues for both families.

They expected us to feed them and even provide transportation to and from the husband's job. This relationship had now begun to hurt my family; they were costing us a lot more than they were contributing. I had to get up early and drop the man off at his job before going to my own job. This got old pretty quickly. They were swift to say how much they appreciated us but continued to take advantage of our kindness. After a few months, the cousin had gotten on my wife's last nerve and tension had peaked fairly high in my home. I just didn't yet understand how to handle this type of dysfunction. I wasn't aware that God was using this situation to train me and develop my understanding of people's behavior. He was teaching me how not to allow anyone to place guilt in the way of my ability to make sound decisions. I finally asked them to leave and only gave them one week's notice. They weren't happy about it, but it sure did feel good to have normalcy back in our lives.

How Can Something So Good Go So Wrong?

1 Corinthians 6:12 says, *"All things are lawful for me, but all things are not helpful. All things are lawful for me, but I will not be brought under the power of any"* (NKJV). We can be addicted to almost anything. Paul stated that he would not allow anything to control him. That's why he wrote these words in his letter to the church at Corinth. He realized that he had the potential to become addicted to anything in this world, but because of his love for Christ, because of who he wanted to be and what God had told him he was to become, Paul was determined to not allow anything to control him. You see, even spiritual folks can become addicted.

The problem with people today is they think that the only things you can be addicted to are alcohol, drugs, cigarettes or other common substances. But humanity is not limited to these addictions alone. Addiction does not just affect the weak minded or those who do not know Christ. I have met enough Christians to know that addiction is also prevalent among church-going, Bible-believing people. Most of these people are not addicted to the top three addictions listed above, but their addiction is just as real. Addiction is anything people seemingly can't live without or feel compelled to have, use or experience in order to relieve pain, pressure, or discomfort. The addictions that we face within the walls of the church are innumerable. First, let's look at approval addiction.

Approval Addiction

The need for approval is pervasive in the halls of Christendom. In the last chapter, I shared how approval stamps an "excellent" on your forehead, just as my grade-school teacher stamped her approval on each of my papers. It rewards a person for work well done. As children, we want people to approve of what we do. If they don't give us the words we want to hear, we react in some way. Most often, children will provide us with an exhilarating taste of a temper

> The addictions that we face within the walls of the church are innumerable.
> ❧

tantrum or the kind of sulk that pouts the lips and creates a clown-size frown. But if you are not affirmed when you begin maturing, then you can begin to doubt who you are. Then the problem of acceptance rears its angry head and compounds the addiction.

Approval addiction shows no gender prejudice. It can come from either parent or another authority figure. The appetite for approval is amplified by specific incidents with our nuclear and extended families that left us on the debt side of the approval spreadsheet. We feel inadequate, less than others, and that we need to make up for it somehow. We often begin to base our self worth on what people think or believe about us. This fans the deadly flame of people-pleasing.

It is rewarding to please people — a smile, a thank you, an outward sign of appreciation all bring a flash of warmth to our emotions. How can pleasing people be so wrong — when it becomes **THE** source of information about your value.

Approval can frame itself in several kinds of pictures.

Picture 1: The Rescuer.

This approval addict needs to be needed. They take on a rescuer persona which is really a false sense of responsibility. For example, you might come across a child that has been abused. The child takes hold of an identity to protect others in the family from the same experience. The child can take on a parental role with the goal of rescuing siblings and perhaps even a parent.

When children who have become rescuers grow up, they feel a weight of responsibility for almost everything anyone else does. They experience guilt when things go wrong, even when it is not their fault. They take ownership of other people's responsibility and feel guilty when these people don't act right. In essence, they save the person who has done wrong from their personal ownership of their problems.

To a rescuer, this seems like a noble cause. Someone tells you, "Oh, you're such a good listener. You listen to my problems and you help me every time." Some of us call it Mother Theresa Syndrome or the Savior Mentality. We make ourselves mini-gods.

Take Julie, for instance. Everybody calls on her to do everything. Everybody in the family calls her when they need some money, when they need a ride, when they need some help, when they need this and need that. Everybody always calls Julie because she's the rescuer — and she does it with such grace! Julie has been known to borrow money in order to loan it to someone because she feels so guilty and responsible that those around her don't have what they need. Who have you rescued lately? Take off the Superhero cape and just be you!

PICTURE 2: THE CONTROL ADDICTION.

An approval addiction can easily translate into a spirit of fear. This fear emanates from feeling like things are out of control and you must bring them in line or no one else will.

Edward Welch gives a few clues as to why we fear people: "1. We fear people because they can expose and humiliate us. 2. We fear people because they can reject, ridicule, or despise us. 3. We fear people because they can attack, oppress, or threaten us."[2] Therefore, you need control. A Control Addiction first manifests itself by us taking such tight control on our own lives that it won't let anyone input or help us make any changes. We take control to the point where we can be assured no one will be able to take advantage of us.

Once you control your own life, you become so controlling that you have to control every single thing around your life. This affects everyone you touch. If you find yourself not in control, you manipulate the situation so you can have some kind of input and feel like you're in control. That's what happens in so many relationships. The wedding takes place and then roles begin to develop. One is the controller and the other is a manipulator and you have a mess on your hands. Or one is a rescuer and the other is a controller then the controller always has the rescuer rescuing. If you think this sounds confusing, try living in this web of a relationship!

These two pictures are just some of the ways in which an approval addiction can color our lives. Whenever we think we must have approval we have a false sense of thinking. Whenever you feel like someone must approve of you or you have to have their approval, you open the door to a great deal of pain and misery because you have become susceptible to

[2] Edward T. Welch, *When People Are Big and God is Small: Overcoming Peer Pressure, Codependency, and the Fear of Man.*

anybody who wants to control you. That's why it is so important to know who you are in Christ.

SELAH:

Pause for just a moment and reflect on who you are. Say these words out loud, "I am a Christian — a little Christ and I belong to Him. Because I am a child of the King, I don't require anyone's approval. I am content to know that my Father in heaven is happy with me." Allow the Holy Spirit to wash away your need to control or rescue or be perfect. Place your self-worth in His hands.

> Whenever we think we must have approval we have a false sense of thinking.

Stop Playing the Tape in Your Head

Have you ever had somebody tell you something was wrong with you and that's all you could think about for the next day and a half? This reminds me of a story about my uncle who played college football. He was from the state of Mississippi and his parents were poor sharecroppers. He was determined to leave the life of living hand-to-mouth for a better life. His goal was to play football, but he was only 5'5" and 160 pounds. Coaches told him he was too short, too light and too slow to play football. My uncle told me how those words kept playing over and over in his head until he became obsessed with his newfound mission to prove them wrong. He labored on the farm, did his chores every morning before school, and then worked with the few weights they had until he transformed himself into a very strong man with a bad attitude. The football team played him as nose guard as he was quick. But he was so hard to tackle that they called him the pig and the name stuck with him all the way to a college scholarship. This is an example of a negative situation that can motivate someone to work for a positive outcome. But most of the time, the enemy uses these negative experiences to turn people into insecure beings unable to perform because of hurtful words from the past.

If it takes only one glance of disapproval or one under-appreciative word to ruin your sense of worth, then you're in bondage. If somebody can just look at you and make you feel like you're not worth anything, if someone can say one debilitating word to you and you feel like a loser, you are in bondage.

If people told you that you were ugly all your life and I were to look at you and tell you how good looking you are, you wouldn't believe me. You might go through life constantly worried about having the latest styles and haircut and car so you can keep up the appearance that you look fine, yet your actions can't disguise the real pain underneath the surface. Often, people who need approval ask, "how do I look?" Though they are looking for approval, many times they still, to your surprise, shove your complimentary words away like dirty linen! They really can't accept the affirmation because their well is so dry and so deep, the only One who can fill the well is Jesus.

People who constantly play negative words through their heads are volatile. This is why we have problems with children who want to get into fights. We must instill within our kids the knowledge of who they are in Christ. Then it will be easy for them to let others call them whatever they want. The remarks don't need to provoke a fight because the child knows and truly believes how senseless they are. The fight occurs when the child feels the mockers may be justified in what they're saying. The fight becomes a means to prove one's self-worth. This is why negative motivation with children almost never works out for the good of the child.

The point is, you have to know who you are. The Lord made me wonderful and beautiful. It doesn't matter what you think about me because I know who I am in Christ and I know God made me in His image. Call me Beaver Teeth. Call me Buckwheat. Call me anything you want to call me, because I know who I am in Christ.

How do you see yourself? Do you have a need to be the most popular one in your office? The need to be popular will steal your destiny. Do you want everyone in your neighborhood to think you are the best family on the block? The need to be accepted by the

> The point is you have to know who you are.

group will cause you to miss your purpose. Do you want your boss to constantly give you words of praise? The need for you to call somebody to approve of who you are will cause you to miss the reason why God placed you in the land.

Have you ever been with a group of people when they began to speak badly about someone? You justify your quiet demeanor in your mind because you didn't say anything negative or join in the conversation. But why are you even with that group in the first place? Do you want to be liked by them so badly that you won't stop them from slandering someone? Hanging with the popular crowd can make you miss your destiny. They are dulling your senses to become insensitive to sin. But what you and I need are people who sharpen us toward our God-given purpose. I need to be with somebody who has enough intestinal fortitude to look at me and tell me the truth that I'm not praying like I need to be. Instead of telling me what I want to hear, they will tell me the truth about myself.

When we try to please people, it seems like everyone wants something different from us. There were times in my life I felt like a vending machine. My wife wanted a good, understanding and prosperous, handsome and submissive husband. At the same time, my children wanted a father who could coach, who was a computer whiz, who was a math major and who knew how to do diagrams. Then my congregation wanted a pastor who was prophetic yet compassionate, anointed but real, available but fully devoted to his family. I felt like each one would come up to me and push the button they chose and I was trying to give

> Hanging with the popular crowd can make you miss your destiny.

them whatever they wanted. Finally, I found myself at the point where I had no life. This was people pleasing to an exponential level!

When God anointed you and purposed you, He didn't want your life to get out of control to where you only live for what everyone else wants. Maybe you have been caught in the "yes" syndrome. You don't know how to decline great opportunities. God doesn't have great opportunities in His will. He has the best opportunities.

When we please people first and give ourselves the leftovers, we feel responsible for everyone. Their mistakes somehow feel like they're our fault; their wrong choices become our burdens. We come to the point that we turn our whole life upside down in order to please somebody. This raises the stress level in our lives to the boiling point, affecting our emotional, mental and spiritual well-being. When someone requests something from us, we need to remember that first and foremost, we need to please God. And if what is being asked of us is pleasing to God, then we will have His grace to do it.

I'd rather be anointed than have your approval. I'd rather God be pleased with me than you to say you're my friend. When it comes to the things of God, it's more important for God to be pleased with me than to gain all the accolades people could give me. Anybody that's really been called to a kingdom purpose will know this is a fact.

There may be times when no one will appreciate you. You've got to be convinced and convicted that what you're doing is from the Lord. It is impossible to please all the people all the time. In fact, you can't please most of the people some of the time. It's not in somebody else's job description to make you happy. Your friend is not conscripted to make your life happy. Even your spouse does not have that in their job description! Your happiness is not found in a child, a friend, a job or a mate. Your happiness is supposed to be found in your contentment in the Lord. Your happiness is found in Christ Jesus and not in people.

> It's more important for God to be pleased with me than to gain all the accolades people could give me.

I will never give anyone enough power to control whether I'm happy or sad. I will never give a man or a woman enough power to control my mood. Nobody should have that much power over your life other than Christ, Himself.

SELAH:

Are there people in your life who seem to be able to control your mood — whether happy or sad? Do you feel like there are times when you can't seem to shake off someone's words, especially if they are negative? Ask the Lord to deliver you from this bondage. Pray for a restoration of your first love — that He would be the source of your strength and joy and not anyone else. Period.)

Does God Really Get It?

At one time or another, most of us have sung a version of "nobody knows the trouble I've seen." But the next line of that song is the best — "nobody knows but Jesus." Is this true? John 15:18 says, *"If the world hates you, you know that it hated Me before it hated you"* (NKJV). Jesus wasn't liked by many people. As a matter of fact, He was not appreciated by most of them. But one day, when He was baptized, the Bible said the heavens opened up. The Spirit of the Lord came down like a dove and a voice from heaven spoke and said, *"This is my Son in whom I am well pleased."* Jesus received His validation, His words of affirmation and acceptance from His Father in heaven. We need to seek the same. You have to come to a point where you have so much confidence in who you are in Christ, you don't allow people to manipulate you out of the will of God.

In James 4:2 it says, *"You lust and do not have. You murder and covet and cannot obtain. You fight and war. Yet you do not have because you do not ask"* (NKJV). We are going about everything the wrong way. We cannot be God pleasers and people pleasers at the same time. We must choose who we are going to serve...now, today...without a shadow of a doubt or procrastinating another minute.

I hope you get so stirred up to the point you can't even rest because you are excited at how you will act tomorrow. Because if tomorrow you go to work and you have the mindset that it really doesn't matter what your co-workers have to say to you because you know that you are a child of God's, made in His image, you will feel victorious over your addiction. You might even get so bold as to put your Bible back on your desk and a Scripture scrolling on your monitor screen. At lunch, you may listen to problems or issues that are brought up and be bold enough to declare the Word of the Lord. You just need to share your testimony about what the Lord has done for you, and what you believe.

We all must come to a point where we don't let the pressure of people around us stop us from becoming who God called us to be. You might even find yourself saying something like, "I'm not going to lower my standard because you don't believe in God; that's your problem." When asked, "You mean you go to church?" you may be quick to say, "Yes. Not only do I go to church, but I'll worship Him right here if you give me a minute. I'll lift my hands and call on the name of the Lord. You better not try me because I'll call on the name of the Lord and bring angels down right around me in this situation." Do you think your fellow workers will freak out over that?!

> We all must come to a point where we don't let the pressure of people around us stop us from becoming who God called us to be.

I have often started up conversations with the servers at restaurants. I would try to find out if they were a believer and, if not, I would begin to speak into their lives. I would say, "If you come close enough to me, I'll touch your arm and the Holy Spirit will then touch you." Now the next part will challenge many of you. I would often say, "When the Holy Spirit touches you, you're going to fall down in the Spirit and start speaking in unknown tongues." Yes, as you can imagine, I've had a few of the wait staff run from the table and refuse to come back to serve me. I am not suggesting we become Bible-thumping radicals. I am saying that we are too timid about our faith and do not take evangelism opportunities seriously because we are afraid of people.

I'm not afraid of my faith. I'm not ashamed of who I am. I'm not ashamed of where God brought me from. People didn't bring me out of the place I was in. People didn't deliver me out of my addictions. The only thing people did was to talk about how bad I was or what terrible things I had done. Nobody delivered me out of it. It took God to do it! And I am sure of this — I am not going back on a God who brought me out of all of my mess. How can I forget about Him after all He's done for me?

Supernatural, Unexplainable, Irresistible Favor

Take a look at James 4:2 again. It says you lust but don't get what you're lusting after; you kill, you desire, you obtain, you fight in war and yet you don't have the things you are fighting for. Then it says something that might be puzzling to you. It says, *"You have not because you ask not."* What are we supposed to ask for? Ask for favor. What does favor do? Favor

51

is not some kind of currency that you can spend on what you desire. "Finding favor means gaining approval, acceptance, or special benefits or blessings."[3] We don't want the favor from people that never satisfies. We want the supernatural favor from God that gives us true joy. God places favor on your life so that when you walk into situations and no one likes you and everybody wants to vote you out, the whole situation suddenly turns around. People look to you and listen to what you have to say. Favor lets you walk into the condemnation of man and hear them say, "I find no fault in the man." That's what favor will do for you.

Ask for favor in choosing your friends. Friendship is when you decide to link with somebody who can add to who you are. You don't need to be linked up with anyone that's subtracting from your life. You don't need to be with anybody that's taking anything away. You have enough takers already. You need people that can add to who you are and what you do.

> Ask for favor in choosing your friends.
> ⚜

Tell God that you want friends who can help you be who He has meant for you to become. If they can't help you toward your destiny, you don't need them as a friend. You have associates who do not add to your life — these relationships are at a surface level. But you can't be in a covenant

---

[3] *Baker's Evangelical Dictionary of Biblical Theology Bibliography.* G. Schrenk, TDNT, 2:743-51; W. Zimmerli and H. Conzelmann, TDNT, 9:376-81, 392-401..

friendship with a person who isn't taking you anywhere. We need friends who are covenant friends.

How does favor work when you are looking for a mate? Don't manipulate. Don't hide the real you. Don't be dysfunctional before you are married! Trust God for your mate. Favor will come as God says, "Yes, this is the one to marry."

Some of us have wished we had trusted Him for our mate, and now it seems too late. We allowed ourselves to get caught up in the emotions and "common sense" that rationalized the relationship. When emotions and rationalization come together, it seems like God is directing us. "I love her so much and she has a good job" — emotions and common sense. However, when you take out the emotional high you are experiencing and unwrap the common sense, you find God isn't in it at all.

But favor works in a different way. Favor isn't about you getting this man or this woman. It isn't about getting a car or a house. It's about who you are and how God is able to use you in the relationship. Favor isn't on an object; it's on the person. Some have explained favor as heaven's currency but it's more than heaven's currency. It's something that's on your life. When you have favor, you walk into a boardroom where everybody there says they're not going to give you the contract and suddenly they approve the contract and don't know why.

Heaven's favor is not predicated on whether you deserve it or not. You can't earn the favor of God. You have a relationship with Him and He bestows grace on you, even when you don't deserve it.

This reminds me of when my wife and I purchased our first home. We were living in a very undesirable apartment that we shared with many other little creatures (of the four legged type). One day on the way to church, we notice a very nice house for sale in a good neighborhood. I stopped and wrote down the address. I proceeded on to church and asked God for the wisdom and finances to take my family out of the horrible living condition we had been in. We had two small children, one being a newborn, and almost no money in savings and no credit history. We made an offer on the house, but it was the lowest offer among two others. The real estate agent took it to the owners anyway. The owner told our agent that she just felt something in her spirit that we were to own her home. So we paid much less than the highest bid and purchased our first home.

The only explanation for the owner's choice was that God gave us favor. When we did not have the money, the credit, or the history to help us, God's favor stepped in and sent us to the front of the line. We were able to move in and take our children out of a rodent-infested environment and into a safe and clean home where our payments were less than the rent we were paying. That is favor.

When God's favor comes on you, those who seem most against you can't resist that favor. Proverbs 16:7 covers this: "*When a man's ways please the LORD, he makes even his enemies to be at peace with him*" (NKJV). It doesn't tell you to fight your enemy. It doesn't say to take matters into your own hands. God doesn't ask you to sharpen your sword or arm your weapons. The verse says that "when a man's ways please the Lord" — now this is a major problem — people provoke us to get us out of the will of God. The enemy lets people into our lives with one intention: to provoke us. The moment they provoke us, we react in a way that is outside of the will of God. Once we are out of the will of God, our ways are no longer His ways and therefore are not pleasing to God. Whenever we get in the will of self, we remove God from the equation and are by ourselves…fighting our enemies instead of enjoying the peace God could provide.

But we don't want to fight by ourselves. We want to know that we have the Lord on our side. The moment we know we have God on our side, it doesn't matter what our enemy looks like. Sometimes we like to sum up the strength of our enemy by looking at him. We might think, "I can take him. I can win this one." And, in essence, we are telling God to stay on the sidelines for this fight. We think we can handle this one. I found out when it comes to the supernatural, I can't

> **We want to know that we have the Lord on our side.**
> ❧

fight anything in my own strength. No matter what I face, I need the Lord to fight with me.

The way to let your enemies lose is to stay in the will of God. It's hard to win against a child of God that's doing the will of God. Jesus said that it's better to have a millstone hung around your neck and be cast into the depths of the sea than to mess with one of God's children [my paraphrase of Matthew 18:6].

When we look at the enemy square in the eye and release the problem to God, He tells us to step aside and watch Him work. When we stay focused on His will and pleasing Him, we don't have the time or the inclination to please people. We need to be careful, because we may be blinded to just how many times we have not recognized the people-pleasing addiction.

SELAH:

Are you in God's favor? Have you felt His favor rest on you in a precarious or negative situation? Have you lifted up your voice and recognized that it was His hand that worked on your behalf? Have you thanked and praised Him with a heart boasting of your God? Try it.

So, How Should We Then Live?

Francis Schaffer, the great theologian, asked the question above and wrote a classic book on this subject. He traced western history and showed how Christianity became watered down though the cultural influences to which it was exposed. His writing inspired many great evangelical movements of our time.

Although I do not purport to have Francis Schaeffer's influence, I do believe what I am sharing in this book can inspire you toward your own great purpose and destiny. We have a choice to live one of two ways: we can live by grace in faith by God's favor or we can live dependent upon our works and our own efforts, trying to do God's job.

Relationships are an important part of life. God wants you to have healthy relationships and anything that's unhealthy will lead to relational cancer. A relationship is not healthy if one person is in control while the other is struggling for approval. I am hoping that you can see how helping someone must have God's stamp of approval. It must be an assignment from Him. But not only that, He must tell you how to proceed. Because God can see the intents of the heart, He knows whether this relationship will be beneficial to you or not. Do you have the same ability as God to see beyond what you hear and see? As your relationship and trust of Him grows stronger, you will hear His voice give you cues as to what to do and how to do it.

But our Father has also given us His Word. Principles abound in the Gospels and Proverbs that help us negotiate the twists and turns of relationships. We must get to know the Word of God to get to know Him. For example, in

Matthew 7:16 we learn how to discern if someone is your friend or not: "*You will know them by their fruits*" (Matthew 7:16a NKJV). An apple tree can scream it's an orange tree all day but if oranges are not coming off its branches, I'm going to call it an apple tree. You can tell me you're saved and you're a Christian all day but if your fruit is mere hopeful ambition, I know you aren't living a Christian lifestyle.

> We must get to know the Word of God to get to know Him.

Another principle from 2 Corinthians 6:14: "*do not be unequally yoked*" (NKJV). This principle is applicable beyond the marriage bond. Relationships, partnerships and friendships all can be unequally yoked. I've had people that wanted to go into businesses with me and had the money to do it...but they weren't saved. My value system and their value system were not the same, so, eventually, the partnership would become problematic. It doesn't matter who you are, where you are or how important the relationship seems. They don't value what you value. What's important to you is not important to them and eventually a clash will occur. This is why I have a lot of associates, but they aren't in strong relationships with me because we are not equally yoked.

If we used just these two principles, we would find a freedom from the need to help everyone and the need to please people. When we become emotionally attached to someone, we must be careful not to let our emotions override the Spirit. Emotional attachments are strong, and when you become emotionally attached to someone, before you know it, you'll find yourself letting your values slip. You will let your guard go down in order to remain their friend.

We wonder why our children give in to peer pressure, but we do the same thing — they're just watching us. They're watching us try to please everybody, so they do the same thing. We must teach them as well as show them that it's all right to say no. When "helping you is hurting me," somehow we must see that we are not the answer. The hurt that we are receiving shows us that the person we are trying to help is really not our friend, nor is he concerned about our well being.

You can still become who God has ordained you to be. Just because something bad happened to you doesn't mean it has to have control over you. Most of the time, we become addicted to something or someone because we want to forget about something. When we push the pain down inside or numb a hurt, we find it will fester later in our lives. But, the God that we serve is a balm in Gilead. He is a healing balm and He can heal you no matter what the hurt or pain. But we have to trust Him and let Him do the work. We need to choose to please Him and not focus on pleasing others. Remember, when a man's ways please the Lord, He makes his enemies be at peace with him. You want to have peace? Let your ways please the Lord. Find favor. Favor will accomplish much!

Questions for Thought:

1. As you take a quick look back on your life, have you ever been addicted to approval? What do you think triggered this kind of addiction?

2. Which picture best describes how you have dealt with the need to please people — The Rescuer or The Controller? What made you choose one or both of these behaviors?

3. What action step do you think will help you move forward toward a life that hears God's will for each relationship you have?

SELAH:

Most of us have some kind of unresolved hurts from expectations that haven't been met or relationships gone awry. Take a piece of paper and list out any names of people from whom you still may feel leftover hurt. Now ask God to put His balm of healing over each one. Ask Him specifically to soften the hurt caused by each of the people on your list. Then rip up the list...give it to Him...and throw the scraps away as a symbol of what He has done for you.

Chapter 3

When Loving You is Killing Me

"You can't buy love, but you can pay heavily for it."[4]
—*Henny Youngman*

Years ago when my wife and I were young parents, we had to hire a sitter for our infant son while we worked, and we were very selective as to who would watch our precious child. Being a minister, I knew most of the congregation at our local church. One middle-aged lady caught my eye in that she had several older children and did not work outside the home. She was very nice, had a great personality and seemingly a nice husband although he did not attend the local church. She wanted to make some extra income so it seemed like a great arrangement for both her family and ours. This worked out well for a couple of weeks until my wife told me that when she picked up our son, the sitter had a swollen face and cut lips. What had happened during the day? I immediately went on high alert. After all,

___
[4] Henry "Henny" Youngman, American comedian and violinist, 1906-1998).

she was watching *my* son. So I started picking him up with my wife and, sure enough, a few weeks later, she had a black eye and bruises on her face and body.

My wife and I asked the lady what happened and if there was anything we could do to help. Of course we all knew what had happened, but she made excuse after excuse defending her husband's actions. I even offered to help her find her own place to live and she told me that she loved him and did not want to leave him. One day when my wife and I showed up, she had been beaten so badly she could not talk, her eyes were swollen shut, and she was in extreme pain. When I ran to the phone to call the police 911 for medical help, she grasped my arm and pleaded with me not to call the police. But after several minutes, I called them anyway. When the police showed up she told them she had fallen down the steps. There was nothing they could do because in those days no charges could be filed unless the victim filed a motion. I could not believe what had just taken place in front of my own eyes! I took my son from her care never to return again. I wondered in my mind how, with that much love in the world, she was loving him while he was killing her. My understanding of love began to change and I grew up in a hurry concerning relationships.

Love is a relative term. One person's love may be another person's idea of a so-so relationship. However you may define it, love is sought after more than any other human emotion. Holman's Bible Dictionary defines love as "unselfish, loyal, and benevolent concern for the well-being of another."[5] By its very definition, you might think it could be dangerous to love…what if the other person doesn't love you back? What if the other person abuses your love? Love is risky business!

How does any relationship get to the point when "loving you is killing me?" When you think about love, do you immediately think of a husband/wife relationship? But love is a part of every relationship on Earth — we either express it or withhold it. Every

> However you may define it, love is sought after more than any other human emotion.
> ❧

relationship has some basis in some type of love. Professionals label those relationships that are unhealthy as "toxic" relationships. According to the Merriam-Webster dictionary, the first definition of toxic is "containing or being poisonous material especially when capable of causing death or serious debilitation."[6] Some poisonous materials, like cyanide, deal a deadly blow immediately. But others can slowly weaken the immune system until we are only a shell of who we were.

Toxic relationships have become commonplace in our society. Just as chemicals can poison us until they either take over our bodies totally or bring death, toxic relationships can bring emotional, spiritual and even physical death. There can be many relationship scenarios that could be labeled as

---

[5] Butler, Trent C. Editor. Entry for 'Love'. *Holman Bible Dictionary.* http://www.studylight.org/dic/hbd/view.cgi?n=3929. 1991.
[6] http://www.merriam-webster.com/dictionary/toxic, access 8/1/13.

"toxic" but I want to look at a few that I have found prevalent in people.

Love is a Many Blundered Thing

The first toxic relationship I want to deal with is one where the dependency on love distorts the interaction between the people involved. A dependency on love may sound okay to us…it may even sound like a goal we should attain to. However, the kind of dependency I am talking about is one where the expected expression of love has become an addiction. These people often seem like leeches, pulling at you from all sides, rarely satisfied with the love given to them. Their picture perfect view of love is actually unattainable. No one or anything could ever fulfill their desires. Their friend or spouse can feel dominated by the expectation that is beyond reach. This is a no-win situation for both people.

> Toxic relationships have become commonplace in our society.
> ❧

Love dependency can get very ugly and possessive. It stimulates jealousy and manipulation. It cuts off the natural flow of life between two people. It is like cutting off the air supply to true love. This is because the love dependent person is obsessed to the point that they only eat, breathe, and think about the love they need. But God says, *"for in Him we live and move and have our being"* (Acts 17:28 NKJV). We need to rely on Him for our emotional needs.

Our emotional needs should not be the judge of how good our relationships are. The controlling party in a love dependent relationship governs the emotions of both people. If the dominant person feels good, then the other person feels good. If the dominant person is having a bad day, then the other person is having a bad day as well. The relationship becomes so toxic that both people do not have lives of their own. Life is based on the response of the other person. But that is too much control to give to anybody but the Lord God.

SELAH:

Do you operate in the manner described in Acts 17:28 — living and loving and having your being in Him only? Take a few minutes to look at a day in the life of you! How quickly do you fall prey to a toxic relationship? Ask the Lord to show you His way of relating to the people that seem to be poisonous to you.

When Anger Makes a Mark

The Bible tells us to *"be angry and do not sin"* (Ephesians 4:26a-NKJV). This verse clearly tells us that anger in and of itself is not wrong. It is the expression of that anger that can manifest in insidious ways. This is the second toxic relationship that can kill us. Listen to Molly's story:

"I was enthralled by the kindness and care John showed to me. I had never met anyone who seemed to know immediately what I needed. He treated me like a queen while we were dating and, after we were engaged, it even got better! Our honeymoon was blissful and the first few months were a happily-ever-after moment. But once in a while John would get angry because I didn't remember to pick up the dry cleaning. He wasn't just disappointed — he was angry. And then he started telling me how many things I did that didn't meet his standard. By year two of our marriage, I was afraid to come home after work. John's barrage of verbal abuse took the wind out of my soul. I know it seems stupid now, but I began to believe what he said…I was an incompetent wife who had no business doing anything but trying harder to make him happy. I felt like I was dead."

The situation with Molly could look like yours with your boss or with a different family member. Anger is one letter away from danger. And the "D" is for death. It can be an emotional death, a spiritual death or even a physical death. The bouts Molly had with John I call "hurt attacks." These attacks come from someone who is in emotional turmoil. They may seem composed and proper, but under the veneer is a festering wound that oozes anger. These kinds of people often have experienced their own set of hurt attacks. They don't know any other way to express their anger. Some have

> **Anger is one letter away from danger.**

learned to stuff their emotions down inside them to where they are so full of hurt, they explode. Think about it. How many people do you know who will talk about physical pain but never their emotional pain? Anguish resides in the faces of many around us but we either don't see it or we ignore it. I believe signs of John's pain existed when Molly and he were dating. She just chose to turn a blind eye toward this and opt for a "perfect" relationship.

Unresolved anger can be torture to a relationship built on trust. And usually the person who is the recipient of the angry outbursts isn't the only one hurting. The perpetrator's conscience denies them peace; they often feel guilt and fear. But the person steeped in anger usually doesn't know what to do. We know where to go when our arm is broken. But we don't know where to go when our heart is bleeding. Instead, we just feed the anger. Anger grows when it is fed.

> Unresolved anger can be torture to a relationship built on trust.

We are created to give and receive love. Hating people is hard work. You have to work hard to stay angry. It takes energy, it burns off your positive attitude, it causes stress so you can't rest, can't sleep, and you wake up the next day and can't focus. Then things seem a little fuzzy — you have to remember why you are angry. You have to remember what she said and you have to focus on it again just so you can be angry all over again. Amazingly, the next day you have to focus all over again just to be angry. When we stay angry,

God will not work on our behalf. When we stay angry, God can't answer our prayer.

When we are angry we can take it out on the cat, get angry with the dog, or get angry with our kids. Even inanimate objects that don't live or breathe can become recipients of our wrath. We get mad at objects because we have a need to feed the anger that's inside of us. But there's no place for anger in a child of God. In Psalm 37, it says: *"Do not fret because of evildoers, nor be envious of the workers of iniquity. For they shall soon be cut down like the grass, and wither as the green herb. Trust in the LORD, and do good; dwell in the land, and feed on His faithfulness"* (NKJV). Let God deal with it.

God can deal with those who seem to persecute us more than we ever could. We may get them back but we won't get even. We may get some satisfaction but we can never do what God can do to them. God may be using the situation to bring them to repentance and, when we take matters into our own hands, we drive them further away from God.

The danger of anger can come in the form of revenge. Now, most of us can't imagine the kinds of revenge that we see on reality TV. These people make a living at exposing just how sick they are. But revenge is often less blatant. We hate people because they have "done us wrong." And so we snub them when the opportunity arises or we make sure they never get the benefit of the doubt. After all, don't we have their history to support our assessment of their worth?

We live out an "eye for an eye and a tooth for a tooth" in subtle ways. Our warped sense of justice believes we have a right to even the score. But hold it right there! Jesus said,

"You have heard that it was said, 'An eye for an eye and a tooth for a tooth.' But I tell you not to resist an evil person. But whoever slaps you on your right cheek, turn the other to him also. If anyone wants to sue you and take away your tunic, let him take your cloak also. And whoever compels you to go one mile, go with him two. Give to him who asks you, and from him who wants to borrow from you do not turn away. You have heard that it was said, 'You shall love your neighbor and hate your enemy.' But I say to you, love your enemies, bless those who curse you, do good to those who hate you, and pray for those who spitefully use you and persecute you"
Matthew 5:38-44 NKJV

Jesus brought to us a more excellent way. Can He really mean this? Something seems wrong with this picture. I would think He'd say, "I'll feel better if they hurt like I hurt." But when has someone else's pain eased your pain? We have a distorted way of thinking that if we hurt those who have hurt us, it will make us feel better, so we go through life hitting back. Who got the last lick? Who got the last word? We exchange insults and sharp comments; we reek of sarcasm. Suddenly, instead of having love fill our surroundings, the atmosphere is filled with anxiety and tension.

The standard Jesus gave us, He kept Himself. He gave everything for a worthless bunch of people who rejected, abandoned, falsely accused, ridiculed, and just didn't get it... and those were His friends! Not only did Jesus tell us to love our enemies, not only did He tell us to bless them, but He said to pray for them that spitefully use you and persecute you. There is the key — prayer. One of the most powerful weapons in your arsenal is the arrow of prayer, but as long as you're angry, you might as well take that arrow out of your quiver and lay it on the ground because you can't use it. The enemy knows you can't use prayer as long as you have anger in your spirit against someone, so the enemy keeps you angry. It's hard to stay angry when you pray for someone. It's difficult to hold a grudge or carry out small acts of revenge when you are lifting a person up before the throne of grace.

Insecurity Is a National Pastime

One of the causes of both the addiction to love and uncontrolled anger is insecurity. My definition of insecurity is uncertainty, lacking confidence, shaky, and a psychological disturbance. Does this describe most of the people you know? A majority of people show their insecurity on a daily basis. Tomorrow, look around at your office and see if you don't see symptoms I describe all around you.

> It's hard to stay angry when you pray for someone.

We can propagate insecurity in ourselves by allowing the weeds of words to take root. If we have firmly put our worth in the Lord's hands, it's like weed killer to the hurtful words. Don't let the way other people treat you determine your worth or your value. We can also encourage insecurity in those around us through our words. Ask yourself— *would the Lord be pleased by hearing what comes out of my mouth?* Remember, these people are His children. You can say a whole lot to a mom or dad but if you say something bad about their child, you have a real problem on your hands. Some of the things you have said to God's children are definitely not pleasing Him!

Insecurity can mask itself so effectively that we think the dominant person in a relationship is the most secure. But when that dominance is manipulation, control, or abuse, insecurity is evident. Two important ways insecurity often expresses itself are when it finds fault and self-inflicts pain. Fault-finding can seem innocent enough. It happens in prayer meetings in many churches when an "issue" with someone is discussed for prayer. We don't know all the facts — we have heard only one side of a story — but we pray as if we are the judge and jury. Can you imagine what God thinks when He hears our slanted prayers? We all have faults...sometimes I feel chief among the brethren in these. But for me to feel better at your expense just creates a new fault.

Pointing out faults kills the glow of a relationship faster than just about anything. When we amplify what someone has done wrong we have not only embarrassed them, we have put them on the other side of an invisible line we have drawn. We are on the right side and they are on the wrong. There's not much room for compromise and communication at that point.

Another indicator of insecurity may surprise you. People who are insecure have often tried just about everything to get noticed. They have done things perfectly. They have marched through people-pleasing hoops. They have thrown adult-sized temper tantrums. But people got tired of those things and they no longer work. So now they try extracting pity from others. They substitute pity for the love they crave. And how do they do this? By self-sabotage. They create problems where there weren't any problems. If this sounds far-fetched, listen to Manny's story:

> *"Barb has always been a beautiful, talented and smart person, but she never believed it. After we were married, I noticed that she always seemed to have a problem. Even the smallest task would multiply into a major event. Nothing seemed to go right for her. And she made sure we were headed for a marital disaster within a few years. After our divorce years later, her mother told me that she had been that way since she was a little girl. If she didn't have a problem, she would create one to gain everyone's attention. She still is creating negativity wherever she goes."*

Manny's story is more common than you think. It might even be your story. Make sure you are truthful, first to yourself.

If God took the time to redeem you, to send His Son to take your guilt and provide the Holy Spirit to continue you in the way toward heaven, how can you be insecure? Unless you believe some lie about yourself more than God. *"Since you are precious and honored in My sight, and because I love you, I will give men in exchange for you, and people in exchange for your life"* (Isaiah 43:4 NIV). Now that's an affirmation of divine proportions!

SELAH:

Declare Isaiah 43:4 out loud. God's view of you is outstanding. That is because He sees you through the blood of Jesus. Be sure to give thanks for His perfect grace that He has provided for your life. No matter which side you are on in a negative relationship, He knows who you really are.

Out of the Ashes

In the movie *Castaway*, Tom Hanks portrays a man stuck alone on a deserted island for a number of years. He finds himself doing things he never did before in order to survive. One of the most intriguing scenes to me was when he had an abscessed tooth. It was full of infection and he tried to doctor it the best he could. But there came a time when he realized the infection was causing his body to become feverish — a sign that he could get very sick and die. It was him or the tooth. The only thing Tom had sharp enough to cut into his gums to extract the tooth was an ice skate. He used the serrated blade on the figure skate as his makeshift scalpel and a rock to hit the blade to get the tooth out. The pain of what he did was so intense, he passed out. But when he awoke, the tooth was gone and the abscess had begun to go down. The thing I admired is his fortitude to cut it in the first place. Sometimes, you have to get rid of something that has been a part of you in order to be healthy.

If a relationship has turned toxic, there is hope. Definitely, without question, there is hope for you. As for the relationship — that depends on first fixing your own issues, and then reassessing the give and take of the relationship from a healed perspective. You cannot fix the relationship without the two people in it changing. And since you cannot fix anybody else (remember the Rescuer syndrome?), you might as well start with yourself.

> Sometimes, you have to get rid of something that has been a part of you in order to be healthy.

Step 1: Consider the relationship as it exists today as dead. Remember, you are killing the relationship in self-defense because it was killing you. Be sure you don't try to fan the smoldering ashes of what once was good. You need to start over.

Step 2: You have declared the relationship as dead but you still have leftover emotional pain that needs to be dealt with. As I mentioned before, begin by praying for the person that has hurt you. Be diligent to pray for the offender each day. The daily exercise of prayer will create a place of healing.

Step 3: Stop the emotional roller coaster. Some of us are up and down on an emotional machine that is out of control. We have butterflies in our stomach when we go over an emotional hill to face certain people. We start tensing up as our mental gears push us toward the top. But we do not have to live here. Find ways to remove yourself from the situation — get off the coaster and allow God to be in control. This may mean excusing yourself from events or situations that tend to get out of control. It may mean we need a "vacation" so we can begin the process of healing. Acknowledging your relationship to Christ is paramount here.

Step 4: Declare Isaiah 61: 1-3: *"The Spirit of the Lord GOD is upon Me, because the LORD has anointed Me to preach good tidings to the poor; He has sent Me to heal the brokenhearted, to proclaim liberty to the captives, and. the opening of the prison to those who are bound; to proclaim the acceptable year of the LORD, and the day of vengeance of our God; to comfort all who mourn, to console those who mourn in Zion, to give them beauty for ashes, the oil of joy for mourning, the garment of praise for the spirit of heaviness; that they may be called trees of righteousness, the planting of the LORD, that He may be glorified"* (NKJV). Declare this for your life every day until you believe it.

Do you notice in the above passage that God is going to give us something when we give Him our ashes….beauty. Only God could make such an exchange. God will take from our hands something that has been burned and completely destroyed and create not just something okay, but something beautiful. When we feel burned and used up, we just need to give those emotional ashes to God. He is waiting to give us something spectacular in return.

Step 5: Make the ultimate effort to forgive. Forgiveness is only possible if you press past the pain and let anger dissolve. When confronted with pain, there's really only three choices you have: you can press past the pain immediately, you can make a decision to allow the pain to linger and say "I'll deal with it later" or you can make the decision to live with it. There's really only one healthy decision and it is to confront it and deal with it now. So let's get busy forgiving.

> My definition of forgiveness is simply this: putting yourself in position to be hurt again.
>
> ❧

To forgive someone may not be a one-time, easy event. This is because our process of healing is gradual; we heal one day at a time and that level of healing gives us the ability to truly forgive, one step at a time.

We spend so much time trying to get what we think we deserve in a relationship and trying to protect ourselves, we never forgive. A good healthy relationship isn't possible because we never got rid of the last hurt before we end up going to the next one in a defensive position — defending ourselves before we get hurt. And if you're defending yourself before you get hurt then you're never really open to love. My definition of forgiveness is simply this: putting yourself in position to be hurt again.

It's just like the relationship between Charlie Brown and Lucy. When Charlie comes to kick the football, she moves it out of the way. He goes flying up in the air and lands flat on his back. Charlie says, "I can't believe you did that." Lucy says, "I'm sorry, Charlie. Come on. I'll hold it this time." Charlie goes running again, and Lucy pulls the same trick so he flies right back up in the air again. Why does he repeatedly allow her to hold the ball for him? Because he forgave her and so he put himself in position to be hurt again.

Growing up, I had sibling rivalry in my house. My mother had four boys and we could get into some nasty disagreements. It sometimes intensified to where the opinion of one brother was forced upon the other. Just like most moms, my mother would catch us fighting and separate us. She'd be angry and tell us she should punish us but instead she would tell us to kiss and make up. I would start crying. She would ask, "Why are you crying?" I would tell her, "Go ahead and punish me now." I really didn't want to make up. I didn't want to forgive. I believe many people are the same way.

Please note that forgiveness is not contingent on the other person's motion to forgive you or even receive the forgiveness you offer. There are no strings attached. Forgiveness is an act of your will and yours alone.

Step 6: Daily attend to the Word of God. When I counsel any married couple, I first ask if they are willing to do homework. Usually they will respond, "Yes!" Then I ask if they are willing to follow exactly what the Word of God says. Another "Yes!" I warn them that if they do not follow what God says in Scripture, I do not have time for them. This is because I believe they cannot move forward without obeying the Word.

In Isaiah 61:3, the oil represents the Holy Spirit. God is saying that He is going to give us joy. We don't need to get our joy from anybody else. Your joy comes from Him alone. What does this joy look like? Imagine a cloak of steel mesh that, when put on your shoulders, weighs you down so much so you stoop over. This is the emotional baggage many of us have. Now, God doesn't just take off that horrible weight and allow us to stand up straight again, He gives us a new garment — one of praise. And praise comes only from a person who is truly free.

Don't Be Bitter, Be Better

Look at John 15:13, "*Greater love has no one than this, than to lay down one's life for his friends*" (NKJV). This is the ultimate sacrifice — dying for someone else. But does this verse describe only physical death?

We all experience hurt — children get hurt, wives get hurt, husbands get hurt. Every time we get hurt, one of two things happens: either it makes you bitter or it makes you better. Not only do we get hurt, but we get hurt again and again. The pattern of how we deal with those hurts can pull us down beyond insecurity and self-image issues. We can let a root of bitterness grow in our hearts to where we can only see the world through our bitter spirits.

Before bitterness can take root, we need to take a leadership role over our own lives. We can be better than taking vengeance and exploding in anger and finding fault with others. Being a leader means we take charge. We take responsibility for our actions and reactions. Leaders are first because they lead the way. We are the first to lead in forgiveness. We are the first to ask for forgiveness. We are first to change the atmosphere around us by loving people when we would rather slap them silly. We are willing to give up our own sense of justice and even the score and promote the other person.

> This is the ultimate sacrifice — dying for someone else.

Being better means we don't have to have our own way. It means submitting ourselves to the obedience of Christ. Psalm 37: 5-7 reminds us, "*Commit your way to the LORD, trust also in Him, and He shall bring it to pass. He shall bring forth your righteousness as the light, and your justice as the noonday. Rest in the LORD, and wait patiently for Him; do not fret because of him who prospers in his way, because of the man who brings wicked schemes to pass*" (NKJV). Don't worry about people that look like they're getting ahead because they are doing wrong. Sometimes the devil wants to show you these kinds of people to tempt you to do the same and veer from God's plan for your life.

Being better means you recognize that not everyone will love and accept you. Jesus even warned His disciples about this when they were to scatter and preach to the world. Matthew 10:14 says, "*And whoever will not receive you nor hear your words, when you depart from that house or city, shake off the dust from your feet*" (NKJV). There are people that are going to see that God's favor is all over your life and they aren't going to like it. Some people may not like the way you're shaped. Others aren't going to like your hair or your nose. Being better means you don't try to change the way God made you just so they will be happy with you.

Being better means we put on love every time we are given the opportunity to do so. Do you have any of those "extra grace required" kind of folks around you? You sigh when you see them coming. When we can put on love with these people, we know we have begun to really learn how to love. You can't have hate in your heart when you love. As James Dobson has said, "Love is a decision." You have to decide whether you will love or not. We need to be like Paul when he says, "*I have been crucified with Christ; it is no longer I who live, but Christ lives in me; and the life which I now live in the flesh I live by faith in the Son of God, who loved me and gave Himself for me*" (Galatians 2:20 NKJV). No more me, myself and I — but the Christ that lives in me.

Questions for Thought:

1. What are things that make you angry? Who are the people who seem to have the ability to make you angry? Think about why these people push your anger forward.

2. Are there areas in your life where you feel insecure? Do you have any ideas as to the source of these insecurities?

3. From your answers to # 1 and #2, this chapter gives ways for you to change your emotional outlook. Which one do you want to use first?

SELAH:

Review the steps that are outlined in the section "Out of the Ashes." Select one relationship or situation that needs work and pray through each step toward freedom.

Chapter 4

When Seeking Him is Fulfilling Me

"The artist is chosen by God to fulfill his commands and must never be overwhelmed by public opinion."[7]

—*Albrecht Druer*

One day while working with my grandfather on his farm, he told me something that has stuck with me all these years: everyone has an opinion but the only one that matters is your own. This reminds me of a very important decision I had to make during my first few years in ministry. As the Bible teaches us, there is safety in the multitude of counsel. I looked for advice from one of my fellow pastors in the community concerning the purchase of a warehouse building. I really respected this pastor's opinion. The warehouse was located in a great location but it was in really bad shape and would take a lot of money to renovate. The pastor advised me to pass on it and look for other options.

---

[7]"Albrecht Durer Quote," www.gotknowhow.com, accessed August 2, 2013, http://www.gotknowhow.com/quotes/albrecht-durer-the-artist-is-chosen-by-god-to-fulfill-his-commands-and-must.

After the initial disappointment of hearing his advice, I began to question the voice of the Lord. Had I really heard Him about this property? That same night the Lord spoke to me in prayer and said to me, "Did I tell you to buy that building or did I ask you to seek someone's approval before you moved on to what I instructed you to do?" The Lord then had me drive out to the warehouse in the middle of the night. The grass had grown high and no lights were on, but I was compelled to follow what the Lord had instructed me to do. As I was trying to get to the front door, my feet became tangled in thorns and weeds. I tried in vain to get loose but could not, so the Lord spoke again and said, "Pick up the cloth on the ground and free yourself." After freeing myself, I went to the front door and found it locked. I said a quick prayer and left before someone thought I was trying to break into the facility. I drove home and sat in the driveway before going into my house. I said, "Lord what was that all about? I feel so foolish!" The Lord again spoke and said, "What is that in your hand?" I still had the cloth in my hand, but it was a towel and on it was written the words "Just say thank you." I began to praise Him right there in my car in the middle of the night. The rest is history — we transformed the building into a beautiful church. Look at God!

You Are in Process

We all have been asked at one time or another, "Who are you?" or "What do you do?" Try asking this question of different individuals in an average day, and you will probably get four types of answers. 1. They define themselves by their career or what they do (I am an attorney; I am a student), 2. They define themselves by their role, class or rank (I am a father; I am well to do; I am a sergeant major), 3. They define themselves by race or ethnic origin (I am Hispanic, I am from Germany) or 4. They define themselves by their belief system (I am a Christian; I am pro-life; I am Independent). Rarely do people actually answer the question as to who they are.

If you know who you are in Christ, then you have an assortment of great answers to that question in the Bible. I am loved and valued, I am a person of worth. I am a child of the Most High God. I am a living witness of the cross of Christ, etc. To answer with a biblical definition of who you are will cut to the chase. People will definitely form an opinion of you once you let some of these words out of your mouth! But that's not so bad…

> When you are a true Christian, transparency is not a threat to your witness.

We know that we aren't perfect. Many people think it is their job to tell us so! But when you are a true Christian, transparency is not a threat to your witness. That is because you are a work in process. God does not just make us, stamp us with the word DONE and then sit us on a shelf. We are born in sin and after we come to Him as recipients of His grace through Jesus Christ, He begins a work in us that uses all

His best tools — the blood of Jesus and the counsel of the Holy Ghost. This allows us to make mistakes and still come back to the wonderful molding hands of the great Potter, glad that we are not left to our own devices.

Just as a caterpillar eats leaves and doesn't look like much, sometimes we are still waiting for the metamorphosis that will make us into a beautiful butterfly. Unlike the caterpillar, we don't wait in a cocoon; we are exposed while we are being transformed. We continue to work, eat, sleep and move closer to the day when Jesus will come suddenly and we will be changed in the twinkling of an eye (See 1 Corinthians 15:2).

Romans 8: 17, 18 reads: "...*and if children, then heirs — heirs of God and joint heirs with Christ, if indeed we suffer with Him, that we may also be glorified together. For I consider that the sufferings of this present time are not worthy to be compared with the glory which shall be revealed in us*" (NKJV). Know who you are. I want you to know and understand that it is critical how we see ourselves. But never ever forget how God sees you. It is through His eyes that we will be judged, not through those of any other person.

If you define yourself from a rank that you have obtained, you will find people comparing your rank to another person's rank. But if you tell them your rank in heaven, "*I am seated in heavenly places with Christ Jesus*" (See Ephesians 2:6), it puts things on a level above earthly review. If you define yourself by your career, there will be people who have known someone in the same career that they don't like for some reason. Then you inherit a bad rap from that person. But if your answer is a biblical statement of who you are to God, they either accept or reject the Scripture — not you. They either believe what God has done for you or they don't...this doesn't have anything to do with your performance; it has everything to do with His. When someone asks me, I can say, "Who is Eugene Reeves? I am a chosen one of God!" For the Scripture says, *"And having chosen them, He called them to come to Him. And He gave them right standing with Himself, and He promised them His glory"* (Romans 8:30 NLT).

If anyone is to pigeonhole who you are and what you can do, let it be God and God alone. Don't let man's labels distract you from the career path God has for you. If you get confused, examine your passion and values. These are things God has placed in you to enable you to fulfill His purpose for you on this earth. Look at your training and experience. Hopefully, many of these were part of God's ultimate plan, but even if they weren't, God clearly says He will use everything for your good, even your trials and tribulation. James 1:2 says, *"My brethren count it all joy when you fall into various trials"* (NKJV). And Romans 8:28 is a favorite, *"And we know that all things work together for good for those who love God, to those who are called according to His purpose"* (NKJV).

When you consider what you would like to be known for, surely you wouldn't want to allow the negative people in your life to write your epitaph. Instead, speak to people about what you do want them to remember about you. If you brag, boast in the Lord! (See Galatians 6:14). We will never be perfect on this earth, but most would want to be remembered as King David and to have said of them "He was a man after God's own heart" or have said of them, "There was no one like her who talked with God face to face" as Moses similarly did. Your legacy begins and ends in the Lord.

> Your legacy begins and ends in the Lord.

The part in between the beginning and the ending is up to you. Will you look to God for your physical needs? Will you look to God for your financial needs? Will you look to Him for your emotional needs? Will you look to Him for the relationships He desires you to have? Will you look to Him for validation of who you are?

SELAH:

Pause to look at the questions in the paragraph above. Start in a spirit of prayer and answer these in honesty before the Father. Let Him know where it is difficult to trust Him and ask Him to help your faith grow in these areas.

In Touch, But Untouched

We are described in the Word of God as living stones. It's a miracle that most of us are alive! But it is even more of a miracle that God says we are being made into those who can offer spiritual sacrifices that are acceptable to the Almighty God, the One and Only. 1 Peter 2:5 says, *"You also, as living stones, are being built upon a spiritual house, a holy priesthood, to offer up spiritual sacrifices acceptable to God*" (NKJV). Remember that God cannot have 99.99% perfect people or things in heaven. They don't qualify. Only the 100% perfect surround Him! So an acceptable sacrifice is 100% perfect. And how can we Christians who still fall into sinful deeds do this? Through the blood of Christ! The Father looks at us through the blood and sees only perfection. What a picture! All the mess in our lives is not just covered but cleansed by the blood of Jesus.

This gives us access to a new dimension on earth. Where unbelievers have a world of three dimensions, Christians have at least four. We are now able to see things from God's perspective, if we choose to do so. We can see why our boss snapped at us when we were just trying to do our job. We know how to pray for her because we see the root cause of her issue. Our boss no longer is our enemy — she is an object of our prayer because she is someone who is not far from the kingdom of God.

We find ourselves using this new perspective when we vote, when we discipline our children, when we volunteer for ministry duties, and we care for the unloving and unkind. Being right with God creates a place where we are in touch with God and in touch with our mission, but untouched by the devil and those he uses to try and take our eyes off the cross.

I'll illustrate with a true story. Horatio Spafford was a wealthy lawyer in Chicago in the mid 1800s. He was a devout Christian with a beautiful wife, four daughters and a son. Tragically, the son died and, shortly after his death, the Great Chicago Fire destroyed almost every investment property Spafford owned. He decided to send his wife and daughters to Europe to give them time and space to recover from the double loss. He said his goodbyes as his dear family boarded the boat. He was to join them later after he finished some business in Chicago. Later, he received news that the ship the family was on had a bad accident and all four daughters drowned. Only his wife survived. Spafford, himself, made the journey to Europe. While on the ocean liner, he wrote the lyrics to the song *It is Well With My Soul*. As you read the words, you will see a man who understands the difference between earth and heaven and allows heaven to reign.

Verse 1: When peace, like a river, attendeth my way, When sorrows like sea billows roll; Whatever my lot, Thou hast taught me to say, It is well, it is well with my soul.

REFRAIN: It is well (it is well), with my soul (with my soul), It is well, it is well with my soul.

Verse 2: Though Satan should buffet, though trials should come, Let this blest assurance control, That Christ hath regarded my helpless estate, And hath shed His own blood for my soul. (Refrain)

Verse 3: My sin, oh the bliss of this glorious thought! My sin, not in part but the whole, Is nailed to His cross, and I bear it no more, Praise the Lord, praise the Lord, O my soul! (Refrain)

Verse 4: For me, be it Christ, be it Christ hence to live: If Jordan above me shall roll, No pang shall be mine, for in death as in life Thou wilt whisper Thy peace to my soul. (Refrain)

Verse 5: And Lord haste the day, when my faith shall be sight, The clouds be rolled back as a scroll; The trump shall resound, and the Lord shall descend, Even so, it is well with my soul. (Refrain)

Spafford understood who he was. The tragedies he faced are unimaginable to most of us and yet he did not let them define who he was. Next to Spafford's challenges, ours may seem rather miniscule. But in Christ, we too, are partakers of everything He earned and desired for us. Therefore, we do not have to be concerned about what someone else's

> Our value is not based on some earthly system or rating.
>
> ❧

opinion is of our value. Our value is not based on some earthly system or rating. Rank, class, race and intelligence are not what we should celebrate. Our value is based upon where we sit; Who we sit with; and why we are there. Heavenly places…God the Father…the blood of Jesus.

1 Corinthians 6:12 says, *"All things are lawful for me, but all things are not helpful,"* (NKJV). As I have shared, I grew up with emotional baggage that seemed like an overwhelming weight of negativity. But even though I spent years developing my self-image based on the opinions of others, I was given moments in time when I had the choice to continue in those feelings and the bondage they brought or to break free. Just because it happened to you and me and we have been through some hard times does not mean these experiences and relationships have to stay with us — in our thoughts and influencing our emotional lives. I believe we can be set free from the judgment and scrutiny of people. No matter what the source of our poor image is, we must step over the debris and find God. When we have found Him, we tell Him, "God, I believe I am your child. I don't want to be dependent on somebody else for my wellbeing. My wellbeing comes from You. And as long as I know You're alright with me, I'm going to be alright with me."

> Man cannot meet our needs. Only God can.
>
> ❧

We are all spirits that have souls that live in bodies. The world addresses these three parts of our being on a warped value system. They don't even understand how these three work together in concert when we are in the heavenly value system. How can man understand his spirit when he doesn't recognize the Spirit of God who makes man's spirit come alive? Man cannot meet our needs. Only God can. He might use a doctor or an accountant to help us, but they are only vessels God has made to help others and us.

Once you have a new heavenly GPS system for your heart and mind, you have forgiveness ready on your tongue; humility becomes exciting; random acts of kindness become purposeful acts of destiny. And the Spirit of the Lord moves in your heart to dance as David danced! You want to dance because there is joy in your life. You are new...not just at the moment of salvation...but every time you step out with the Lord.

Second Corinthians 5:17 says, "*Therefore, if anyone is in Christ, he is a new creation; old things have passed away; behold, all things have become new*" (NKJV). Here's the special thing about God — God loves us because He wants to love us, not because we did anything to justify His love.

SELAH:

Begin to thank God for His act of salvation so that you could be a new creature. Praise Him for being a God of love, a God of eternity, a God who supplies every need. Then worship Him for loving you just because He wants to. Plain and simple...but very profound.

Our God is One of a Kind

The world has a problem with a God who seeks to save mankind. Since the beginning of man, people have created gods who asked and demanded and asked more and demanded more and never seemed to be satisfied. Such is the god of Buddhism, Hinduism, Taoism, Islam, and so forth. *Yahweh* is the only God who loves people just because He wants to. And when those people let Him down, He supplied the way to come back to His arms. He did it all and we just receive. With opposing viewpoints of gods, it is easy to see why Christians are singled out and are different from all others. Can you see why your value system is so far superior to any other value system? It isn't one out of many choices — it is the only true system. So why would Christians allow themselves to be defaced, defamed, and deceived by people's inferior ways of thinking? But that's what many of us do.

> Yahweh is the only God who loves people just because He wants to.

God sees everything we've got hidden. He knows everything about us — there's nothing He can't see. All those nasty ways, all the old filthy habits, all the thoughts we have in our minds — He sees and knows all of them and still chooses to love us anyway. You don't understand how good and powerful that is. When we see flawed merchandise, we take it back or ask for a discount. But when God came looking for us, He wasn't expecting us to be perfect. He didn't suddenly discover we were flawed. We didn't catch Him off guard. He knows us because of Jesus and He just comes along side and wants to help us. He is amazing in His love toward us.

How many times have you not had money in your pocket, but you had some money in the bank? So if somebody had asked you, "Do you have some money?" our first inclination would be to say, "No, I don't," because you didn't have any money on your person. But if somebody were to ask, "Are you broke?" you would say, "No, I'm not broke, even though I don't have any money on me. I know that there is a place that has some money in my name."

You might be in a place where it looks like you're emotionally broke, you might be in a place where it seems like you don't have anything of value, but all you have to do is remember that Christ has paid for you. It is in the bank. All you have to remember is where your name is written. You have your name on the deed. If you believe you are bad, if you believe you are a sinner then guess what will happen — you will continue to be what you tell yourself. But I want to tell you what I have discovered — that just because this is what I used to think about myself does not mean that's what I'm going to continue to believe.

Romans 8:31 says, "*What then shall we say to these things? If God is for us, who can be against us?*" (NKJV). God is on my side. When we played baseball in P.E. at school, two people were picked as captains by the teacher. These captains then took turns picking the people who would be on our team. I was talented enough that I got picked either first or second, but woe to the poor guys at the end of the line. The captains would look at each other and know they had to select one or the other, but they really didn't want either. These boys didn't do well at baseball and everyone knew it. Everything was based on who could help us win and we only wanted the best on our teams.

But you see, God is on my team. It doesn't matter who else is on it or how many star players I have; with God all things are not only possible, but He eliminates the opposing team. With Him I win just because He's there. Here is a paraphrase for Romans 8:31, "With God on my team, did the other team even show up?"

Take this parable a little further. When God is on your side, you don't have to worry about their designated hitters. When the other team comes to the plate to bat, they can swing but will not even hit the ball. They can try and do damage to you by trash talking and intimidation, but it's as if they aren't even there.

> Another unique aspect of our God is that He speaks to us.

Another unique aspect of our God is that He speaks to us. He puts thoughts that are different than our earthly, carnal thoughts into our minds and hearts. Many Christians wait for prophets to come to their churches so they can get the Word of the Lord. However, when I search my Bible, it says that the prophet speaks what God has already said to you (see

Deuteronomy 18:20-ff). In other words, the prophets are really to either confirm something God has already said, or bring words God has shared with you forward because you haven't seemed to hear them yet. God wants us to desire prophecy, but He also wants us to hear for ourselves. Allow yourself to get trained to hear from God's Spirit and not your own mind. Learn to discern the truth from the pseudo-truths that either your carnal mind generates or someone else speaks to you. This will give you clear guidance about any area of your life you bring under submission to Christ.

Be confident in who you are in Christ. This will spill over to your interactions with people who used to give you "hurt" attacks and those who once had power to control your way of thinking about yourself. Someone can shoot negative things at you, but you are only wounded in the fray if you put down the armor God has given to you.

One of the greatest ways we can get rid of old habits and ways of thinking is to worship. This is because when we are in the presence of the Lord, we will be changed, 100% guaranteed. Let's look at a picture of worship from the Old Testament. The story of Naomi, Ruth and Boaz is particularly beautiful to me. There are many lessons we can learn from this story, but I want to focus on worship. Boaz is a type or a shadow of Jesus Christ to come. Naomi represents the Holy Spirit and Ruth is a type or shadow of the Church. Naomi instructed Ruth uncover Boaz's feet while he was sleeping and to lay down at his feet. At midnight, Boaz got up, looked down at Ruth and asked who she was. When life comes at you in the midnight hour, if you have enough worship to get at the feet of Christ, you can get His attention and He will look at you and ask you who you are that He should pay attention to you. Ruth answered that she was a relative of Boaz's and he was her kinsman-redeemer. When Christ asks you who you are, you can answer enthusiastically that you are a child of the King. This qualifies you to wake up your kinsman-redeemer who is Jesus and receive His undivided attention.

Ruth didn't identify herself as the Moabite widow who hadn't believed in Yahweh until she came to Israel. She didn't need to tell him the mistakes she made or issues she had. She told Boaz the relationship she had to him. When we come to worship at Jesus' feet, we tell Him who we are in God — His child. The devil is trying to get you to be known by the mistakes you made. He wants your whole life to be classified by your mistake instead of your miracle.

> When we come to worship at Jesus' feet, we tell Him who we are in God — His child.

But we are not mistakes. We are miracles. We receive the benefits of being children of the King of all kings. Romans 8:17 says, "*and if children, then heirs — heirs of God and joint heirs with Christ, if indeed we suffer with Him, that we may also be glorified together*" (NKJV). Once who we are is settled, we can focus on the kingdom. He gives us strategic relationships to move us forward and to move the other person forward. He allows us to enjoy even the relationships that result in iron sharpening iron because we have His perspective on where we are going. We know what boundaries to set up and what barriers to pull down. We no longer need delivered from people because we negotiate the roadmap of relationships with His voice guiding us. We can become agents of His love just as "little Christs" are supposed to be. Carry on!

Questions for Thought:

1. As you have read this book, have you been able to sort out some of your relationships as to whether they were helpful or hurtful? How will you foster those that build you up? How will deal with those that do not function well?

2. Find places in the Bible that describe the children of God and those who are believers. Write down those descriptive words (ex. bought with a price, beloved, heirs of salvation, etc.) that are used to describe those who walk with God. Use this list every day to remind yourself of how God sees you.

3. Make a note on your calendar 3 months from now to check in and see how your relationships have changed… where they have been strengthened….where you still need work to keep from falling into traps.

SELAH:

Consistently develop your life of private worship. Steal away from the activity and quiet your spirit so God can fill you with

His joy, His peace and keep you steadfast on your unique place in His kingdom. Enjoy the journey!

Chapter 5

A Parting Word

When we walk in relationship with Christ, He will free us from all bondages from the past, through the blood of Jesus. *"Believe in the Lord Jesus Christ and you will be saved (healed and delivered), you and your household"* (Acts 16:31-RSV-Parentheses mine). There is power in the name of Jesus — the power to heal, deliver and set us free from any type of bondage that the enemy has us believing about ourselves. More than anything else, the Lord's purpose for coming to Earth can be summed up in His desire to restore relationships both with the Father and each other. Our families should have strong relationships, not become fractured or broken collections of people just existing together. We need to desire relationships as God created us to depend on each other, not to live as an island alone. It stands to reason that if God desired that we have meaningful relationships, Satan has spent endless hours trying to destroy the intimacy that should flow out of those relationships. He replaced intimacy with hurt and brokenness.

I believe that the Church is a collection of families, and if Satan can create broken families, he can cause a church to feel broken. The enemy knows that Christ said "*Upon this rock I will build my church.*" Therefore, if Satan cannot destroy the Church directly, he desires to destroy the families within the Church. Our local churches need to be connected as families and not just gatherings of people in an association.

Multitudes brought their loved ones to Jesus for healing and deliverance. The books of Matthew, Mark, and John are filled with examples of family and friends bringing their loved ones to Christ so He could meet their needs. This is supposed to continue today; if you have a relationship problem that seems to be out of control, remember there is healing in the name of Jesus. You should love yourself enough that you will no longer allow anyone, regardless of relationship, to abuse you. God loves you so much that He was willing to send His only Son to die for you. Why would we allow anyone to abuse someone that is so very important to God? Love God, love yourself, and love people...but only associate with those who respect you.

—Eugene V. Reeves